Valerie B. Johnson

A Glimpse of Old Ledbury

by David Postle

Published by
Amber Graphics
Bideford House
Church Lane
Ledbury
Herefordshire HR8 1DW

ISBN 0 9510684 2 3

Printed by
The Amadeus Press Ltd., Huddersfield

Contents

Acknowledgements

The majority of the photographs in this book are from my own collection which I started some years ago and which has been growing ever since. There are, however, a number of pictures which have been specifically loaned for inclusion in the book, and for their kind permission to reproduce them, I am very grateful to Miss Leonie Tilley, Mr. Derek Maisey, Miss Sue Hubbard and staff of the Hereford County Record Office, Robin Hill and the Hereford Library, Mrs. Nancy Paice and the staff of the Ledbury Library (with thanks also for the use of their local newpaper records), National Monuments Record, Mrs. M. Shotbolt, Mrs. M. D. Notley, Mr. C. F. Ballard, Mr. J. C. Boyd, Mr. M. Hale, Mr. J. Gough, Mr. M. Handford, Mr. R. Smith and Mr. R. Holland.

The Market House was built in 1633 and has brick panels in between the timber framing. It is supported on sixteen substantial posts of oak, some of which were joined by wooden rails. Many people would pass the time of day leaning on these rails, and they still bear a polished look.

Introduction

As the title suggests, this book contains a glimpse into Ledbury's past. In truth it is only a fleeting glimpse. The hardest part of compiling this book has been deciding not which photographs to put in, but which photographs to leave out.

There is a legacy of photographs of the town and surrounding area which portray life as it was. This is largely due to Luke Tilley & Son and more recently J. C. Smith, both old-established family businesses.

In the first twenty years of this century, John Tilley used to carry his heavy glass-plate camera around with him, recording scenes and events. Newpapers did not carry photographs in his day, and many of his pictures were published as postcards, partly as a supplement to the newspapers, but also as a means of communication between people not fortunate enough to possess a telephone. In that 'Golden Age' of postcards, from the turn of the century to the First World War, the photographer would take pictures of the local street scenes, buildings, events, people and even bizarre accidents. There was virtually no subject that was not recorded on postcard. Nearly 900 million of them were posted each year, and it was only after the First World War that the importance of the postcard as a means of communication was to diminish with the more widespread use of telephones and improved transport.

It has been very difficult to select photographs to include simply because of the large number available. I have therefore decided to concentrate on that Golden Age, although one or two others are included where they illustrate particular points of interest. I have also been selective in the number of subjects I have chosen to illustrate, so that some detailed information can be included on each within the limited space available. This book is therefore presented in a series of cameos - just a glimpse into some of Ledbury's past. The photographs that I had to leave out will have to await a further volume!

November 1988

High Street, the Market House and the Barrett-Browning Institute in 1903.

Ledbury

Ledbury is an ancient market town serving a large rural area. Some of its buildings are very old - for example, the church is thought to date back to the eleventh century, and many of the half-timbered properties that can be seen on a walk around the town are from the Tudor period. The town was the scene of fierce fighting in the Civil War, some remnants of which are still visible today. It has a patron saint, St. Katherine, it was on the mail routes in coaching days and boasted some coaching inns, it has a remarkable Market House on stilts, and it had a lot of inns. Many of them have disappeared today, names such as The King's Head, The Swan, The Sun Tavern, The Crown & Sceptre, The Bell, The Green Dragon, The Vine Tap, The Fox, and The White Lion being just a memory of past drinking.

During the first twenty years of this century, you could also drink at The Feathers, The Prince of Wales, The Royal Oak, The Seven Stars, The Ring of Bells and Ye Olde Talbot, amongst others. You could buy groceries from F. W. Taylor, the India & China Tea Co. or Bebbingtons, buy fish from L. Crossley, buy coal from John Meates or John Haines, send or receive parcels from The Royal Oak (Great Western Railway agents), The Feathers (Midland Railway agents) or Tilley & Son (agents for Sutton & Co. parcel deliveries). You could have your boots repaired at Brays, Milwards or Merrits. There was always a tremendous choice available, much more so than today.

There were outside interests for people to pursue. You could play golf at the nine-hole course behind Conigree Wood (annual subscription, ladies one guinea, gents two guineas), join the Territorials, Scouts or Girl Guides, ride with the Ledbury Hunt, join the Ledbury Coal Club, play cricket or football, badminton or cribbage, or you could spend your time reading at the Barrett-Browning Institute. You could read all about it in the weekly local newspaper.

Ledbury was a vibrant town, and during these first few years of the century, a great deal of change was taking place, particularly in the field of transport. Cars were becoming increasingly used by those who could afford them, and many of the following pictures show the sometimes uneasy combination of the motor car with the more traditional mode of transport, the horse and cart.

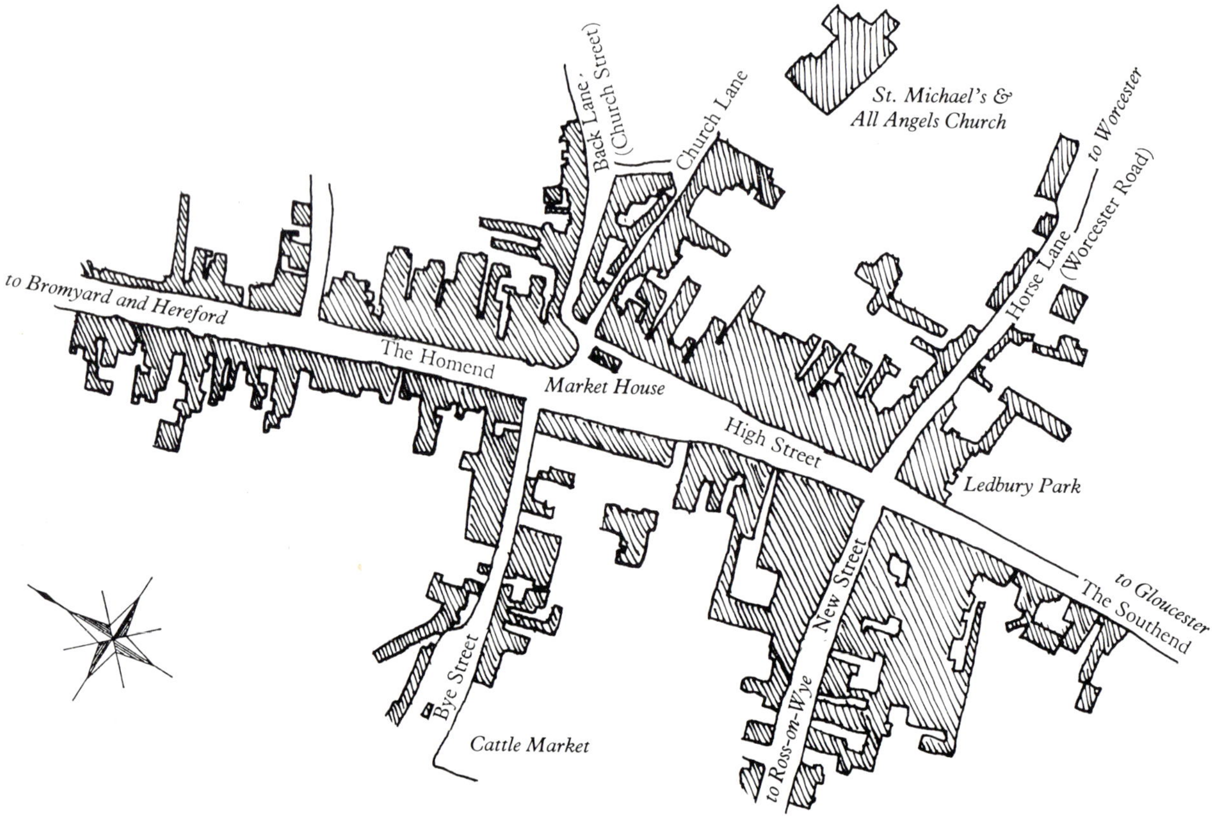

The Market House

The market place with a few cars and vans, but certainly no traffic congestion. The telephone box on the left has long since been moved.

Extensive repairs were carried out to the Market House in the 1860s, and the wooden scaffolding can be seen around the building. The interesting black and white building on the extreme left facing the Market House was demolished before the turn of the century.

High Street looking towards the Top Cross. Compare the herring-bone timber framing of the Market House in this picture with the other side of the building shown on page 4. One of the impressive features of the High Street was the decorative balcony that each building had at first floor level.

High Street in the snow. St. Katherine's still has its metal railings which were later recovered as part of the war effort.

R. Edy's shop at the end of Church Lane. It was taken over in 1902 by the India & China Tea Company, and at present houses the Ledbury Craft Centre.

High Street

High Street looking from under the Market House. The timber framing of the Feathers Hotel has recently been exposed. There is obviously some sort of boot sale taking place under the Market House.

St. Katherine's Hospital with spectators. Although there has been a hospital since the thirteenth century, the present building was erected in 1822, with an extension being added in 1866. Each inmate received a ton of coal on St. Katherine's day, and clothes on alternate years. Until the late 1800s, the male inmates wore a blue broad-cloth coat with brass buttons. The gardens in the foreground are now part of St. Katherine's car park.

The Feathers Hotel with its half-timbered facade hidden by plaster which was removed about 1908. It used to be a coaching inn on the Aberystwyth to Cheltenham mail route. A small room in the hotel was used as the Corn Exchange. A horse and cart conveyed visitors to and from the railway station. The visitor who owned the front car with its chauffeur waiting had no need of this service. He had come from Manchester.

Next door to The Feathers Hotel were the fishmongers McDonald & Co. They sold fish, fruit, poultry and ice, and were licensed to deal in game. Every day from Tuesday to Saturday, the shop's fishcart left Ledbury at 9 a.m. to serve outlying villages. Mr. Lawrence Crossley ran the shop and the business became known as L. W. Crossley around the time of the First World War. The premises are now occupied by a Building Society.

This photograph of High Street was taken at 11.00 p.m. on July 1st, 1908. Although it was taken on a long time exposure, hence the white streak of a passing bicycle with its light, the sky at that time of night was bright enough for the photographer to record the scene in as much detail as if it had been daylight. One theory put forward was that this was the effect of the Aurora Borealis, not normally seen in this area. Some experts referred to it as just a particularly bright afterglow caused by unusual atmospheric conditions. It had not rained for fifteen days beforehand. Whatever the reason, V. W. Meacham, the chemist, can be clearly seen to the left of Webb and Sons. W. L. Tilley's premises at No. 17 (with the garage sign) still has the rendering on the wall, which was removed in 1924.

This photograph was reproduced as a postcard in 1905. It is in fact two photographs joined in the middle. If you look closely, the same car appears on both sides of the road, as indeed does the gentleman walking out of the clothing shop at No. 23 High Street. CJ180 was a 12 h.p. red and black Gladiator and was only a few months old when this photograph was taken. Behind the steering wheel is Mr. W. L. Tilley, the owner. Up the alley by the side of Tilley's shop was 'Boodle's Teeth', where you could go and see D. Gore Boodle & Co about your teeth every Tuesday between 11.30 a.m. and 6.30 p.m.

TILLEY & SON
TILLEY
BEVAN
HORTON
W. H. HORTON
LEDBURY GUIDE
CJ 80

The view from the Top Cross in the 1870s. On the left is Luke Tilley's original shop, and between that and the Feathers Hotel is Webbs bank. They later became part of the Capital and Counties Banking Co. The premises were rebuilt in the late 1880s. At the corner of Bye Street, the old tannery still stands. The Feathers Hotel horse and cart awaits some passengers to take to the station.

A local policeman stands watching the animal traffic at the Top Cross.

This view of the Top Cross is believed to have been taken on the occasion that the Herefordshire & Worcestershire Agricultural Show was held in Ledbury, between June 7th and June 9th 1911. The Showground was a meadow on the Hazle Farm out on the Ross road. The flags and decorations were provided by Tilley & Son, and a local collection raised £618.14.6d., some of which was donated to the hospital.

Worcester Road

Looking down Worcester Road towards the Top Cross in 1904. Worcester Road was once called Horse Lane.

R. & C.B. Masefield's premises on Worcester Road. They were solicitors and still occupy the offices. The building beyond was demolished when the town's new police station was opened in 1954.

The Avenue, Worcester Road. The message on the back of the postcard is most frustrating. It reads 'I expect you know who this is', but elaborates no further!

The Southend

Gypsy caravans in the Southend alongside the wall enclosing the Park gardens.

The Southend in 1904. Behind the Royal Oak Hotel was the Royal Hall, an assembly room which was capable of holding 500 people. It was licensed for stage plays and frequently used for performances by local actors. It was also used at one time for boxing contests. The Ledbury Free Press Offices are behind the delivery cyclist, and the notices on the wall state that the paper 'contains more local and general news that any other paper published in the district.'

AN OLD HOUSE
LEDBURY

The gardens of the Park in 1903. The 'summer house' has gone and this part of the grounds was sold for housing. Horse Lane Orchard now occupies the site.

Opposite top: This was the residence of Lord Biddulph, once called 'The New House' but now called 'Ledbury Park'. The building dates back to 1590 and is historically important. Prince Rupert made his headquarters here in the Civil War and Queen Victoria once stayed at the house. The railings down the Worcester road have been removed, but otherwise the building looks just the same today. The policeman does not!

Opposite bottom: The rear of the Park. The gate onto the Southend can be seen in the garden wall. Today, the premises are occupied by H. J. Chapman, stationers and printers.

New Street

Hamptons Shoe shop was on the corner of the Southend and New Street. This photograph was taken about one hundred years ago, when you could buy shoes for between 5/9d and 10/6d.

New Street about 1880. The large building on the left was the premises of the Ledbury Mineral Water Company which no doubt supplied the three Inns visible in the picture -The Vine Tap, The Old Talbot and The Bell. In the late 1920s the building was converted to a private residence, which it remains today.

The Old Talbot Inn about 1880. Later photographs of the building when the rendering had been removed show a window to the right of the projecting bay. Like the Feathers Hotel, this was once a coaching inn and was built in 1596.

The dining room at the Old Talbot Inn has one of the finest examples of old oak panelling in the country. It still survives today. It was the scene of fighting between Prince Rupert's men and Cromwell supporters during the Civil War, and the bullet holes can still be seen in the panelling.

New Street in 1904. Ye Olde Talbot has lost its rendering and gained a new sign. Mr. W. L. Tilley poses in his car, a 3 ½ h.p. dark green and red Benz dog cart, and a crowd looks at the scene from The Top Cross.

Some of the staff and cars of George Hopkins & Sons, outside their premises in New Street. The building with the curved nameboard remains, but the other buildings were recently demolished and replaced by a supermarket.

A pause for four horses outside the Vine Tap.

The Biddulph Arms in 1920 offering good food, accommodation and stabling. It has obviously been extended within the last few years. The publican, Mr. John Rouse, poses in the doorway. This whole area has changed. The photograph was taken from the Ledbury to Gloucester railway line, which has been closed since 1959. Now the foreground is covered by the new by-pass, constructed in 1988. The name of the inn has been changed to the Full Pitcher Hotel.

Church Lane

Church Lane about 1900.

The top of Church Lane in the snow in 1908. Just before the Prince of Wales is a small bill posting station owned by Tilley & Son. The snow partially hides the fact that home-brewed beers were available at the inn.

Church House in the 1880s, in a rather dilapidated condition. It was acquired by the Rev. Maddison-Green in 1891, and he spent a lot of money restoring the property. The building on the other side of Church House was a tannery.

The west front of Ledbury Church with its beautiful Norman doorway. The present building dates from 1140, and is one of very few churches in the country to have a tower detached from the main building. The photograph was probably taken in the 1880s, as by 1900, the fencing had been removed.

Bye Street

At one time, there were buildings down the middle of this part of Bye Street. Now, not only have they gone, but also the buildings on the middle left which have made way for the fire station and Masefield Close.

The Tilley's Posting Station in Bye Street. One very interesting advertisement is for 'the Event of the Season' to be held for two nights only at the Royal Hall. There was a grand re-production (sic) of the final for the English Cup between Newcastle United and Wolverhampton. Prices for the night's entertainment were 6d. or one shilling.

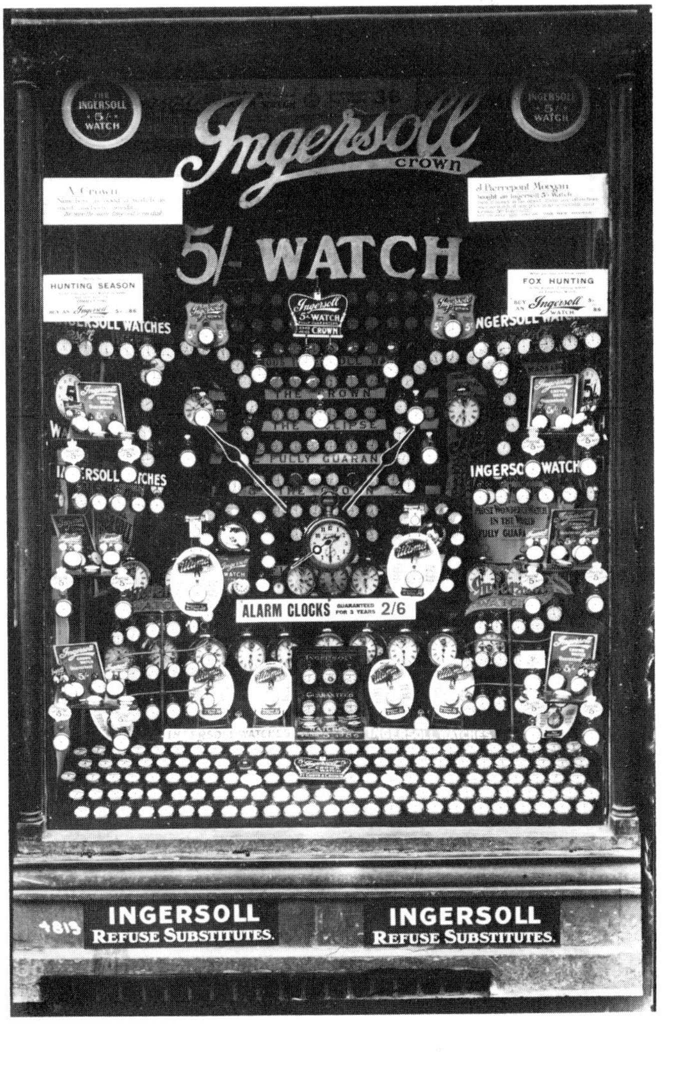

The Homend

The shop window of No. 18 The Homend which is almost totally full of Ingersoll 5/- watches and 2/6d. alarm clocks. Tucked right at the top of the window is an advertisement for the Ledbury lever watch, costing 3/6d. and guaranteed for five years. The shop was owned by Mr. Charles Berkley, and it is still a jeweller's shop today.

Market day as a farmer drives his cattle up the Homend. The New Inn Hotel is on the left hand side, next door to William Marklove, the grocer. This shop is now a betting office.

Looking down the Homend towards the town centre. The Homend certainly had its fair share of inns. Both the Fox Inn and the Swan Inn have long since disappeared. The left hand side of the street has changed considerably. The houses with steps have been replaced with modern flats, and Bank Crescent has yet to be built.

A similar view in the 1920s, with modern transport starting to make an appearance. The Swan Inn has become the Swan Cycle works. The two cars have come a long way - the front one from Oxfordshire, the rear one from Brighton.

William Madders & Son's grocery at Nos. 86 and 88 The Homend. Hams and cheeses are displayed in the one window, soaps and starches in the other. No. 86 is now a launderette, whereas No. 88 was demolished by a lorry running into it in the 1970s. The premises were rebuilt and are now occupied by a gun shop.

Two views of the Homend taken in fairly quick succession. The cameraman has caught the cattle and sheep being driven into town passing the railings of the Baptist Church on the left. To the far end of those railings is the White Horse Inn, and to the nearer side is William Harris's ironmongery shop displaying baskets, trunks, pots, pans and buckets. The bicycle belongs to the photographer who cycles towards the town centre to catch the procession further down the street.

Westhill

Westhill was the home of Major Palairet. These photographs show the interior of the house as it was in the early 1900s. To the right are the hall and staircase, and at the bottom of the page is the smoking room.

The Markets

The right to hold markets in Ledbury was vested in the five lords of the manor by an old charter of Queen Elizabeth. You could buy anything on the streets from clothes to pots and pans, to sheep and horses. The livestock market was held every second Tuesday in the month when the local farmers used to drive their animals along the road to the town centre. Horses and cattle were paraded in the Homend, and sheep and pigs were penned in the High Street around the Market House. There pens normally took up so much space that it was not possible for two carts to pass - traffic congestion is nothing new!

In 1887, the Ledbury Markets and Fairs Co. Ltd. was formed with the express purpose of removing the livestock market from the streets. The Company purchased three acres of orchard between New Street on the one side and Bye Street on the other, on which Mr. Gray, a surveyor from Tewkesbury, laid out a new market. A road was constructed to join the two streets and iron pens were constructed for the animals. The site cost £1,000, but the Company sold off about half the land it had acquired for building purposes, which brought them £800. The new market accommodated 250 beasts, 700 sheep and 400 pigs, with room for expansion if necessary.

Agreement had to be obtained from the five lords of the manor for the new market to be built. Lady Henry Somerset was the first to be approached, and she was keen to see the scheme go ahead. The other four followed her lead and gave their consent.

The new market was opened on Tuesday 12th July 1887. For the first auction, all animals were admitted free. Normally there was a toll ranging from 6d. for a horse and for a bull (on condition that it was tied up) to 1d. for a sheep. The auction started at 11 a.m. and was very well attended by people from as far apart as Birmingham and Bristol. After the sales, a public dinner was given in a large marquee that had been erected on the site. Over 300 people had bought their 2/- ticket for the dinner and they enjoyed the catering provided by Mr. H. Best of the New Inn. Six months later, the local newspaper was reporting how successful the new market had become.

The centre of Ledbury continued to see markets on the streets for many years after the animals moved. Even today, there are regular stalls permitted beneath the Market House. The cattle market remains very much as it was and continues to serve the local farms.

High Street prior to the opening of the new cattle market in 1887. The pens which were used to keep the sheep in some semblance of order are placed in the middle of the road ready for market day.

The new cattle market between Bye Street and New Street in the early 1900s. Parked at the back of the market are a Showman's caravan and a steam organ belonging to H. Strickland & Son of Worcester. The auctioneers were W. Manton & Co., later to be Lomas & Anthony, whose offices were in New Street.

The fish stall under the Market House in 1907.

High Street at the turn of the century and through traffic about to have difficulty getting through the crowds.

A later photograph of the market place. Cars and buses have joined the horses and carts.

A clothes market by the Market House in 1904. The notice on the cabinet behind the front stall is advertising for recruits to join His Majesty's Army. The gas for the lamp was supplied by the Ledbury Gas, Coal and Coke Co. Ltd. whose premises were down New Street.

The Street Market, including C. H. Pritchard's Penny Bazaar directly in front of the Market House. Mr. J. Davies, the ironmonger, advertises his business with a very large kettle hung over his shop. This kettle became a familiar sight in Ledbury for many years.

PARR

Schools

By the turn of this century, the public elementary schools were controlled by managers appointed by the Herefordshire County Council and the Ledbury Urban & Ledbury Rural Parishes. The Boys' School was in the Homend, where the headmaster was Mr. G. W. Paul. The school was built in 1867 and enlarged in 1894 to accommodate 230 boys. It was built on a site given by Mr. John Martin, and included a master's residence.

The Girls' School was in Back Lane, next door to the Infants' School. Miss Hooper was in charge of about 170 girls in the former, Miss Adams in charge of about 162 children in the latter. The girls' and infants' schools were built about 1850 by W. J. Miles esq.

There were other schools in the town. Miss Ballard, for example, ran a young ladies' school at Abbey House in the Homend. In the Southend was the Elizabeth Hall School for girls, commonly referred to as the Cookery School. Miss Hall had left enough money in the early 1700s to provide for a schoolmistress and twenty-four children, and a schoolmaster to teach eight of those children to write. School dinners were provided here even in the nineteenth century. The children would take a halfpenny with them and would receive pea-soup on Monday, rice-pudding on Tuesday, Irish stew on Wednesday, boiled beef and suet pudding on Thursday, and pea-soup again on Friday.

The curriculum included all sorts of domestic crafts as well as reading, writing and numbers. The school was rebuilt in 1910 and later became known as the New School of Domestic Economy. Another young ladies' school was run by the Misses Russell at Bank House, and there was also the Russell Endowed School where Mr. F. W. Wade was the headmaster.

Sometime in the latter part of the last century, there had been a Grammar School in what is now the Heritage Centre in Church Lane, but it was not until 1923 that another Grammar School was established, this time at Upper Hall. After the Second World War, a further secondary school was built at Mabel's Furlong which has recently joined with the Grammar School to become the John Masefield School.

Apart from the Masefield School, none of the others mentioned have survived.

The interior of Ledbury County (Girls) School which was in Back Lane. The site is now occupied by a new housing development.

The old Grammar School in Church Lane is the building on the left. Although it was called King Edward VI Grammar School, it was probably in existence long before his reign. He bestowed upon it a permanent endowment to provide free education for four boys.

Some of the pupils pose outside the Abbey School in the Homend. It was a school for young ladies, but somehow a young boy managed to squeeze into the photograph. The school continued until the beginning of the Second World War.

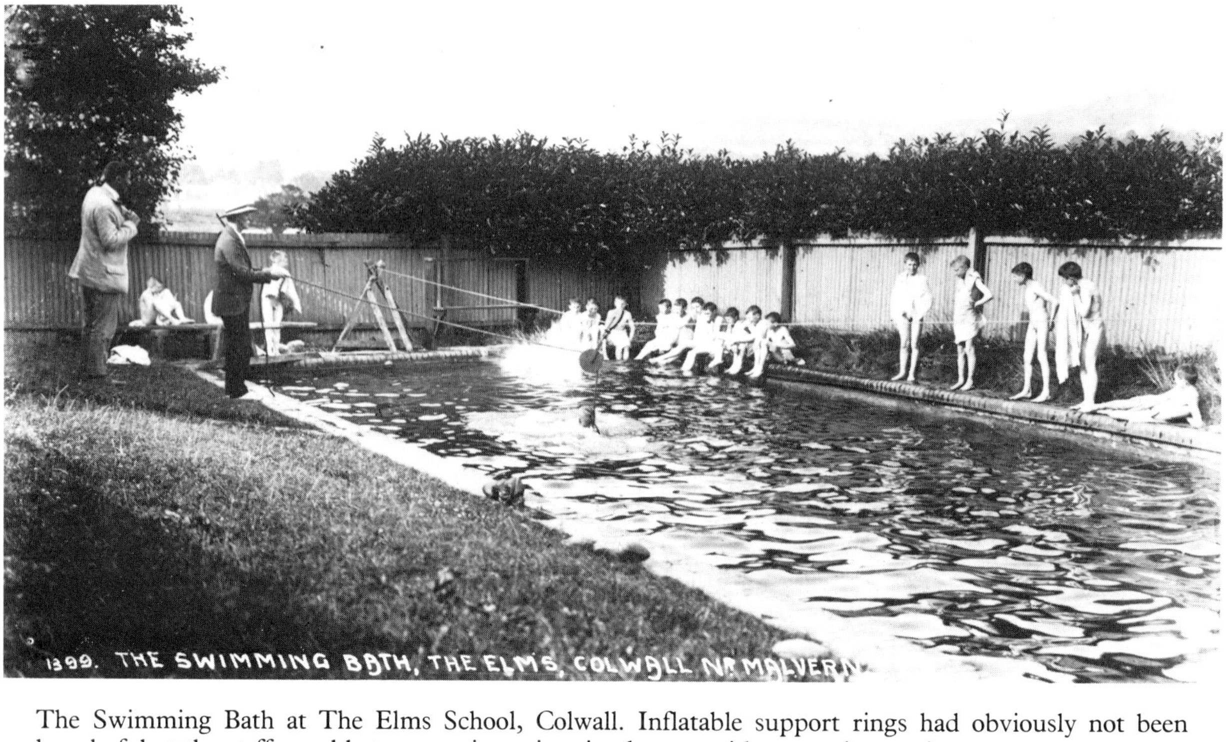

The Swimming Bath at The Elms School, Colwall. Inflatable support rings had obviously not been heard of, but the staff are able to supervise swimming lessons without getting wet!

The Boys' school in the Homend. Just to the right of the school is the headmaster's house. Both were demolished in 1986 and a luxury block of retirement homes now stand on the site. Before the buildings were demolished, the bell tower was lifted off by a crane and taken to the new junior school at Longacre where it now stands as a memory of the old classrooms.

The pupils of the Boys School pose for their form picture in 1899. Mr. Paul the headmaster is in the middle of the third row.

Two Local Writers

Ledbury has been home to three renowned poets - William Langland, Elizabeth Barrett-Browning and John Masefield. A few miles away, in Bosbury churchyard, the author Edna Lyall is buried, close to the old cross which she wrote about in one of her books.

Edna Lyall was the sister of the Rev. Robert Burges Bayley who was the vicar of Bosbury from 1897 to 1906. She spent many happy days visiting her brother, particularly in the spring. She had written several books which earned her a reputation not only as a novelist but also as an atheist and a follower of unpopular causes. Her novels were often based on her own stance, and she was frequently the subject of attacks by her Victorian critics. One of her most interesting novels was *In Spite of All*, a historical novel describing the Civil War in Herefordshire, particularly around the Ledbury and Bosbury area. In the book she describes the saving of the old cross in Bosbury churchyard from being broken up during the Civil War. It was sitting by this cross that Edna Lyall corrected the proofs for *In Spite of All*. She died in the cold winter of 1903, and in accordance with her wishes, she was buried in Bosbury churchyard. The stone cross bearing her name was sculptured by Charles Hill and Sons of New Street, Ledbury.

Edna Lyall was only 46 when she died. Her ashes were scattered and an Iona cross of red sandstone bearing her name was erected next to the old cross which had featured in her novel *In Spite of All*.

The Barrett's house at Hope End. It is, perhaps, fortunate for the family that the stringent planning controls of today did not exist in 1809!

Elizabeth Barrett-Browning was born in 1806 at Coxhoe Hall, Durham, and three years later moved to Hope End, just north of Ledbury, where her father had bought the estate on which he proposed to build a brand new house. The house that already existed was soon incorporated into Mr. Barrett's new mansion, becoming part of the stable block. The architecture of the new house was not exactly native to nineteenth-century Herefordshire. With its Turkish minarets, solid concrete walls and cast iron tops, it took six years to build, and internally boasted many peculiarities, such as the provision of windows above the fireplaces.

It was from this house that Elizabeth Barrett-Browning started writing her poetry, much of it based on the beauty of the surrounding countryside. In 1832, the family left Hope End for Sidmouth. She never returned, saying that 'it would be like seeking to bring together a plucked flower and its broken stalk'. Elizabeth spent the later part of her life in Italy where she died in 1861.

In 1873, Mr. C. A. Hewitt built a new house at Hope End, and he demolished the house erected by the Barrett family. It is reputed that he resorted to powder to blow up the building. Mr. Hewitt's house was also destined to be short-lived, for on 2nd April, 1910, the house caught fire and was destroyed, causing over £50,000 worth of damage.

Some of the firemen take a break to pose for the camera. This postcard was written by a gentleman who was a guest at the house. He writes: 'The stairs are entirely gone, they had caught fire at the bottom owing to a portion of the burning roof having fallen into the space below and setting fire to the couch and portions of the molten lead splashed on us as we went down so we were not a moment too soon in getting out of the house'.

This view of the aftermath of the fire shows the St. Day room, the Bay room and the Drawing room windows, through which you can see part of the lake and the drive to the house. It also shows how completely gutted the building was by the fire. There are no floors or roof remaining.

The Barrett-Browning Institute

A Mr. William Russell who lived at Woodlands, Parkway, first suggested the idea of erecting a memorial to Elizabeth Barrett-Browning, one of three famous poets to be associated with the town, and he pledged £50 towards the cost of building a clock tower. A public meeting was called on January 27th 1890 to discuss the proposal. It was very well attended and Mr. Russell's ideas were enthusiastically received. A committee was established under the chairmanship of Mr. W. A. H. Martin to oversee the project and to raise funds. Mr. C. W. Stephens was appointed the Hon. Secretary. At this time, the proposal was for the clock tower to be built in the High Street opposite the tower of St Katherine's and in the summer of 1891, a 'mock-up' of the tower was erected. Later that year, Mr. Stephens announced that he had acquired the property on the corner of the Homend and Bye Street which comprised two shops, stables and a tan-yard. He offered the site as a substitute to the High Street, and this was gratefully accepted by the Committee. The building plans had grown in concept since the original scheme and designs were invited for the clock tower and an institute to contain a lecture room, reading room and a caretaker's flat. Forty-five entries were received, and the winning design came from Mr. Brightwen Binyon, an architect from Ipswich. George Hill, a local builder, submitted the lowest tender and he started work in August 1894. The building was completed almost a year later at a cost of about £2,330, including fixtures and fittings

Sadly, Mr. Russell died before seeing the works completed, but his widow donated £150 for a four dial striking clock in his memory.

The official opening of the Memorial Clock Tower and Institute took place on Thursday January 16th, 1896. Mr Henry Rider Haggard, a famous novelist, was presented with a golden key on which there was a portrait of the building. He used this key to unlock the door and declare the building open for public use.

In 1938, the Barrett-Browning Institute extended its role and housed the public library. John Masefield, who was then Poet Laureate and another famous poet connected with Ledbury, performed the ceremony on November 11th. The public library is still in the building.

The shops, stables and tannery at the corner of Bye Street and the Homend which were demolished to provide a site for the Barrett-Browning Memorial. Just further down the Homend was the Temperance Hotel and the Central Café.

High Street with the 'mock-up' of the proposed clock tower before Mr. Stephens acquired the site on which the tower now stands. Elizabeth Barrett-Browning no doubt would have been more impressed with what was actually built than with this scheme.

Progress after three months' work. This photograph shows the Barrett-Browning Institute under construction in November 1894.

The Barrett Browning Institute after completion. By chance the pair of horses pulling the cart towards the photographer were owned by George Hill whose company built the Institute. His premises were just out of sight up the Homend.

The Railway

The railway came to Ledbury largely thanks to a local man, Stephen Ballard from Colwall. He had previously worked on the Herefordshire & Gloucestershire canal and he teamed up with Thomas Brassey, a very wealthy and well respected railway engineer, to complete the line from Worcester to Hereford. There were three major engineering difficulties which had to be overcome. The first was the tunnel through the Malvern Hills at Colwall where the rock was so hard that only a few feet of progress were made each week. The first locomotive to actually work on the Colwall side was hauled over the Hills by horses, and was used to haul spoil from the tunnel.

The tunnel was eventually completed in July 1860, nearly a mile long, but it was to prove troublesome. Less than a year after being finished, it had to be closed for a few days because of a fall of rock beneath an airshaft. The condition of the tunnel continued to deteriorate from then on, and it was reputed that some trains came out of the tunnel with bricks on the roof. Not all engines had an enclosed cab for the protection of the driver and fireman, and these poor gentlemen must have feared for their safety on passing through the tunnel. Eventually, the Great Western Railway replaced the tunnel with a new bore through the Hills and this was opened in August 1926. During the war the disused tunnel was used for storing torpedo warheads. The problems seem to have been solved, and the second tunnel is still in use.

The Ledbury tunnel was not so difficult to bore, but it was always very narrow and badly ventilated. Drivers and firemen of steam trains sometimes used to lie on the floor of their cab with damp handkerchiefs over their mouths struggling for air to breathe. Even today it is not possible to get out of a train by the normal outward-opening doors if it should become stuck in the tunnel. The guard's inward-opening door is the only means of escape.

Ledbury viaduct was constructed using bricks that were manufactured on site. It is reputed that about 300 girls from Staffordshire carried the clay on their heads to the brick kilns. The whole project required over five million bricks and was completed in the summer of 1861.

The line had been opened to Malvern Wells from Worcester the previous year, but it was not until September 1861 that the line was officially opened through Ledbury to Hereford.

Shortly afterwards, the canal which Stephen Ballard had helped to build was leased to the railway company which eventually closed it. A new railway line was built following the course of the old canal from Ledbury to Newent and Gloucester. The canal was filled in and a large part of it was used for the trackbed of the railway which was opened on 27th June 1885. Receipts did not live up to expectations, however, and the line through Dymock and Newent was closed in 1959.

Today the line from Worcester to Hereford is still open, but it has been reduced to the status of a single track branch line from Malvern Wells through to Hereford.

Some of the engineering staff who helped to build the railway between Worcester and Hereford. Stephen Ballard is seated in the middle.

This 1860 view shows the Colwall end of the tunnel being driven under the Malvern Hills. A horse is just bringing another load of spoil out from the bore.

Ledbury viaduct under construction in 1860. The contractors had their own small railway system at ground level for transporting materials to the hoists, and this can be seen just behind the fence.

When work on the line to Gloucester was started in 1881, a lot of earth was required for the embankments. The contractors excavated most of it from around the tunnel, and in doing so, shortened the original tunnel by about seventy yards.

During the construction of the Gloucester branch in 1881, a bridge was built over the main Hereford road, and this photograph shows it under construction. Although the line closed in 1959, the bridge still survives.

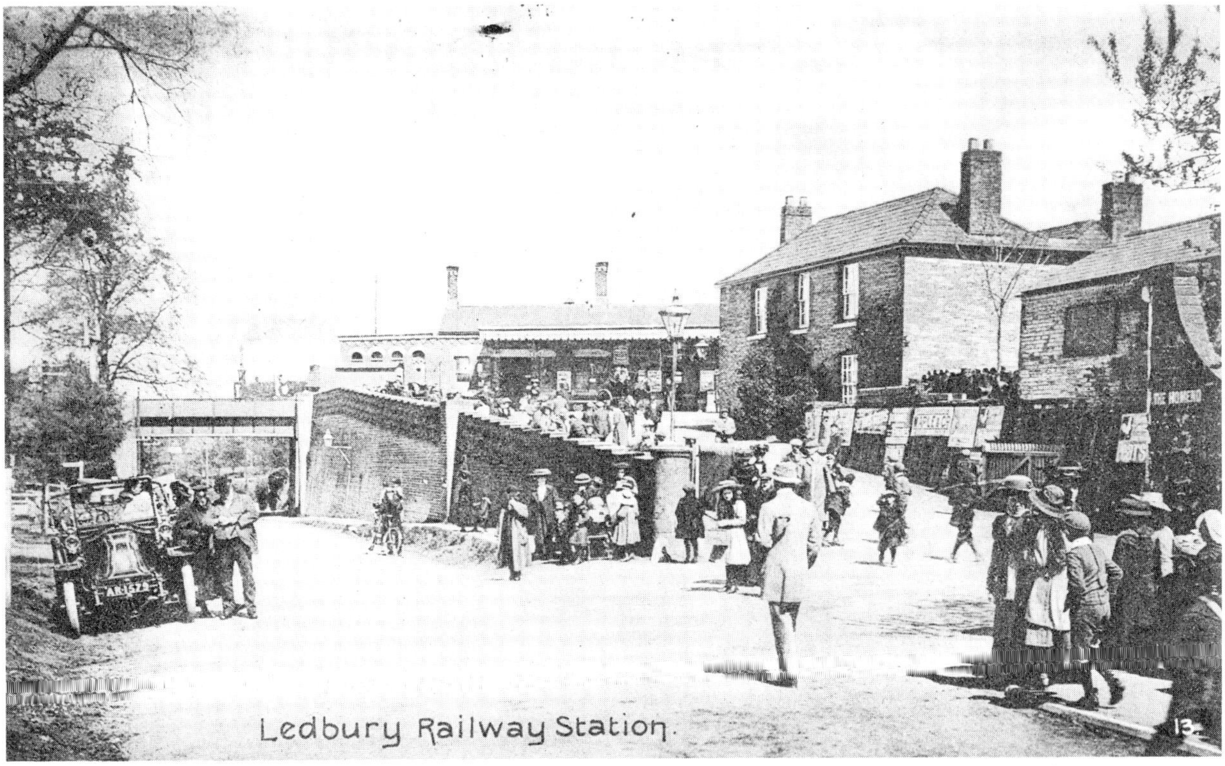

Ledbury Railway Station in 1910. There is a lot of genuine activity at the railway station, but it does seem as though the locomotive crossing the bridge has been added to the picture for effect. It was not uncommon for postcard publishers to amend their pictures by either adding or removing detail.

Ledbury Town Halt on the Gloucester branch. The bridge under the street has now been demolished, and the tall building on the left was wrecked in an explosion a few years ago.

Ledbury Station from above the tunnel in 1906. The station is a hive of activity. A Gloucester bound train approaches from the tunnel whilst a train for Worcester is just drawing into the platform. A third engine is shunting in the yard. The yard and the big shed are full of trucks and there are several horses and carts to be loaded with goods to deliver locally.

The Tilley Family

Luke Tilley was one of five brothers, Matthew, Mark, John and Peter being the others. He came from Dorchester to Ledbury in 1869 to set up business as a stationer, newsagent, bookseller and printer. The first building he occupied was No. 23 High Street, now the premises of Oakes and Son, the tailors. Sixteen years later he acquired No. 16 High Street on the other side of the road and moved the business to where it is still trading.

Luke Tilley and his wife had two boys and two girls. John joined his father's business in 1903, bringing with him several ideas for new ventures. It was from the camera of John Tilley that many of the views taken in this book originate. He opened a photographic studio up the alley behind the shop and took many portraits of local people. Perhaps his greater interest, however, was the towns, villages and countryside around Ledbury. He travelled far and wide with his camera and box of heavy glass plate negatives. He would often use his means of travel as a feature in his photographs, so you may see his bicycle propped up against a wall, or his car parked in the street. Quite often, his wife would also appear in the foreground.

It was from these photographs that John Tilley started producing postcards to become one of the most prolific local publishers. They were postcards of almost every possible subject - from the street scene, to disasters, to acting performances, to shop fronts and so on. In addition to the postcards, John Tilley introduced a bill posting service. Not only did he print posters, but he was the lessee of all the private posting stations in Ledbury and the surrounding area. There were walls with advertising posters in Bye Street, the Homend, at the bottom of the station drive, and further out at Trumpet and Hollybush. Mr Taylor was employed as the bill poster.

Brother William Tilley operated from No. 17 next door where he sold motor grease, lubricating oil, spark plugs, gaiters and other motor accessories. He was the official stockist of Dunlop tyres, and the sole agent for bicycles with such illustrious names as Sunbeam, Royal Enfield, Raleigh, Singer, Triumph and Humber. He repaired bicycles on the premises and even took old bicycles in part payment.

The hire of bicycles, mail carts, perambulators and even invalid chairs was all carried out from No. 17. In the cattle market, in what is now Coles Knapp salerooms, Will Tilley used to have his repair garage for motor vehicles. He also ran his car hire from there.

In 1924, John Tilley acquired No. 17 from his brother and undertook a very extensive refurbishment of the property. It is one of the oldest buildings in Ledbury, dating back to about 1530 - hence the name given to it, Tudor House.

John Tilley who took many of the photographs in this book.

John Tilley's next venture was to establish the Tudor House library with a large stock of the newest novels by popular authors. You could borrow either one, two or three books at a time, and you paid either 21/-, 31/6d. or 42/- per annum for the privilege. The library lasted into the 1960s until the buying of books for stock became too expensive, and the competition from the free public library too much. His Master's Voice and Columbia Gramophones, and a large number of records were later added to the stock in the shops, and became a very important part of the business.

Although John Tilley died in 1926, the Tilley family connection remained. His daughter Leonie with help from Derek Maisey, her nephew, ran the business until her retirement three years ago. Tilley Printing is still trading and producing *Tilley's Almanack* yearly and *The Illustrated Guide to Ledbury*, much the same as it has been for decades, but the shop has now been taken over by Finlay & Co.

No. 23 High Street where Luke Tilley, who is standing in the doorway, started business in Ledbury. He moved from this shop in 1885 to premises across the road.

Tilley & Son's shop at No. 16 in 1903. W. L. Tilley's cycle shop can be clearly seen next door.

No. 17 High Street was in very poor condition when John Tilley took it over, and very extensive repair works were required. The whole building was gutted, revealing the old timber frame. George Hill & Son of Ledbury did the work and this photograph shows the shell left when the rendered facade was removed. Health and safety regulations with regard to scaffolding were obviously not as stringent then as they are today!

Tilley & Son's shopfront at No. 16 High Street. There are a lot of postcards for sale, and looking at those of local events, this photograph would have been taken about 1908.

Newspaper delivery girls, but who, when and where is unknown.

Tilley & Son not only traded in Ledbury, but also travelled to shows with their wares. This event is believed to be the Three Counties Show.

The advertising hoardings at the bottom of the railway station drive in 1911. All the posters are advertising events in 1911 except for the one that the bill poster is pretending to paste up which is dated 1910. One can only hope that Mr. Luke Tilley, who is sitting in the back of the car, has not noticed.

Some of the radios and spare parts for sale in the shop.

One of the cars that W. L. Tilley made available for hire. He himself sent this postcard, writing 'Please let me have as many petrol cans down as soon as you can. I want Bowleys mostly. W.L.T.'

W. L. Tilley's new garage by the cattle market. From left to right the cars are a 1910 blue 14/16 h.p. Darracq Landaulette, a 1908 dark blue 18 h.p. Darracq tourer, a 1909 red 10/12 h.p. Darracq G.P.O. mail van, and a red and black 1910 15 h.p. Star mail van.

Changes

Ledbury is rich in architectural history, with its narrow streets and half-timbered buildings. Until recently, the town had fortunately been spared some of the excesses of modern development, and the centre of the town remains very largely as it was at the beginning of this century. The major changes that have taken place have been the loss of fields to housing development. Areas such as the 'square field', Bye Street, where the junior football team once played, have long since disappeared under bricks and mortar, but these have been additions to the town, rather than a replacement of existing buildings.

Nevertheless, there have been examples of demolition and replacement. Butchers Row was perhaps the best known, a row of old houses which stood in the middle of High Street and which was demolished in the early 1800s. One of these houses survives and is now located in Church Lane, housing a small museum. Here are a few more examples of buildings that no longer exist.

Back Lane, which is now known as Church Road. The view is looking towards the Market House. The houses on the right were demolished and St. Michael's, a building of warden-supervised flats, was opened on the site in 1974.

The Homend. The steps were needed on these houses because the land rises very steeply at the rear of the buildings and the ground floors were built well above street level. Turner Court, a number of flats with a resident warden for elderly people , was completed in the late 1970s on the site once occupied by these unusual houses.

The premises of David Smith, a building contractor, was opposite the Boys' School in the Homend, and supported one of Luke Tilley's posting stations. The site is now occupied by Spicers.

Bye Street looking towards the Homend. Only the balcony of St. Katherine's and the café are left today. The buildings in between have been demolished to make way for the entrance to St. Katherine's car park. Similarly, the wall on the left has been knocked down to give access to a car park.

Bye Street. If you stand in the same place as the photographer, you will see Masefield Close and the fire station, with the swimming baths and community centre in the distance. You can see these houses in their setting on the photograph of Bye Street on page 26.

View from above the railway bridge in Bye Street. Not only has the railway bridge gone, but so have most of the buildings in the foreground, the one on the right being demolished by a gas explosion. The Ledbury Youth Centre now occupies the area in the middle of the photograph.

A country residence near Kilbury Camp of which there is no trace today.

Hop-picking

At the turn of the century, many of the bigger farms around Ledbury grew hops, and the oast houses in which the hops were dried were a very distinctive feature of the local countryside. Generally, the crop was harvested in early September. It was a certain sign of September approaching when the town experienced a rapid influx of itinerant labour, together with all their belongings, or so it seemed. The hop-pickers would often come by train from the Black Country, or from South Wales. They would get out of the train at the nearest station to the farm, whether it be Ledbury, Ashperton or Stoke Edith, and pile their belongings on the platform. The luckier ones would be met by a horse and cart from the farm, onto which they would struggle with their baggage to their place of employment.

This was the annual holiday for a lot of the pickers, earning a little bit of money at the same time as being away from home. It was a family holiday, so that father, mother and children would all be out in the fields. It was a very different way of life from the urban poverty from which many came, and sometimes they would keep the local constabulary busy, particularly after a night's drinking.

The Great Western Railway treated this annual pilgrimage with some trepidation. They would often provide the worst rolling stock they could muster. They would probably have used cattle wagons if they could have got away with it.

In addition to the itinerant workers, many local people went to work in the hop-yards. The contrast in appearances was often very marked with the locals seemingly dressing in their Sunday-best and the ladies wearing large colourful hats.

Having loaded the carts with their luggage, the hop-pickers make their way down the station approach on their way to the farms. Some of the Ledbury townsfolk have come to watch the proceedings.

The carts look almost overloaded as the group of hop-pickers wait to have their picture taken before setting out from the station towards Bosbury. At least the women and children seem to be assured of a ride.

The hops were taken back to the farm by horse and cart. There would seem to be a definite division of responsibility between the men and the ladies with their children.

A contrast between a family on holiday and a few local people. In most hop yards the bines were grown up poles. The hops were hand-picked and put in the crib. The pickers were paid for the amount of hops they had actually picked, and were often paid in tokens which were redeemable only against purchases made from the farmer himself. On the picture below, Mrs. Dance is standing on the left at the end of the crib.

The oast house was where freshly picked hops were taken to be dried. At the bottom, a coke fire would be burning and the hops would be placed in a tray about twenty feet above the fire. The warm air from the fire would rise to dry the hops and escape through the conical ventilators at the top. The air would be thick with the unmistakeable smell of hops. The smell would also cling to the clothes of the pickers and would be noticeable from several feet away, even to a not very sensitive nose.

Sports

Most sports were played in or around Ledbury in the Edwardian era. There were football teams, senior and junior, a cricket team, people played tennis and croquet, and of course in such an area of this there were the country field sports.

The Ledbury Hunt was always very well attended, both by spectators and participants. The Hunt would meet at different locations around Ledbury, quite regularly at inns such as the British Camp Hotel, Colwall Park Hotel, The Walwyn Arms, Much Marcle, and The Beauchamp Arms at Dymock. On Boxing Day they would meet in the town itself and any traffic that wanted to travel through Ledbury had to wait until the Hunt had moved off. The whole town seemed to turn up as part of their Christmas festivities to watch the hounds arrive from their kennels by the railway station, and the beautifully groomed horses parade with their immaculately turned out riders.

During the 1909/1910 season, the Ledbury Hunt had the services of two masters, Captain Warren Peacocke, of Linden House, Ledbury, and Sir George Bullough of The Down House, Redmarley, where a lot of the meets were held. In that same season, forty-four brace of foxes were killed in 110 hunting days. In April 1910, Captain Peacocke resigned to leave Sir George the sole master.

The Ledbury Hunt meeting at Colwall Park Hotel on February 12th 1910. Colwall Temperance Hotel is the left hand building and the Post Office is on the right.

The crowds come to see the meet at the British Camp on March 5th 1910.

The hounds of the Ledbury Hunt were kept in kennels just off the Bromyard Road, immediately behind the station which can just be seen in the background.

Ledbury Juniors football team in 1907. There were two teams, a Thursday XI, captained by Mr. B. Maddox, and a Saturday XI, captained by Mr. F. Hocking. Their Headquarters was the Central Cafe, and their ground was at Jubilee Meadow, between Gas Works Lane and the Ross road, where they pose. The Ledbury to Gloucester railway line passes at the back of them. By 1910, they had moved their ground to Brickyard Meadow.

This is believed to be Eastnor football team at the turn of the century. There is a marvellous variety of methods used to keep their shorts up!

Badminton and putting behind The Lawns in the Homend. The gardens of this large house used to stretch down to the Ledbury to Gloucester railway line, but now there is a car park, housing development and a swimming pool on the land. Today, The Lawns is occupied by Barclays Bank.

In only its second provincial meeting, the R.A.C. visited Ledbury on July 11th, 1908 at the invitation of Lord Biddulph. Between fifty and sixty cars arrived which was less than expected, but there were competing attractions - for example, the Fromes Hill hill climb - and the weather was bad. The cars lined up under The Park wall along the Southend from three o'clock onwards and the 200 guests visited The Park grounds where the Aloe tree was in blossom. This tree was reputed to blossom only once in a hundred years. The catering for the occasion was done by Mr. E. H. Hopkins of the Royal Oak Hotel.

Fund-raising

Fund-raising is not just a recent activity. The Edwardians were good at organising large scale events in order to raise money for worthy causes, and here are four examples: for the Herefordshire Choral Union, the Cottage Hospital and Dispensary, the Church Room building fund and the Red Cross.

Choral Festival, 25th June 1908

Every three years a festival of Parish choirs was held in Ledbury Parish Church under the auspices of the Herefordshire Choral Union.

Over 250 choristers from Hereford Cathedral, Almeley, All Saints (Hereford), Eastnor, Eaton Bishop, Kington, Ledbury, Much Marcle, Storridge, Tarrington, Wellington Heath, Weston under-Penyard and Yarkhill arrived in the town by train, bus, cart and foot.

Rehearsals were held in the morning under the direction of Dr Sinclair, the organist at Hereford Cathedral. Lunch followed in the Feathers Assembly Rooms before the festival itself at 2.45. A collection was held in the church which raised £5 in aid of Choral Union funds. After the service, most of the choirs returned to the Feathers Assembly Rooms for further refreshment.

Congregation and choristers mingle in the churchyard after the festival before going to the Feathers Assembly Rooms for tea.

Hospital Church Parade, 19th July 1908

Despite there being a successful Church Parade the previous year, the hospital found itself short of funds, principally due to the large number of patients that had been admitted during the last twelve months.

The procession assembled in Mr. Bray's field by the railway station shortly after 4.30 p.m. and walked down the Homend, High Street and the Southend, stopping on the way at the Hospital, Lower Cross and Upper Cross. It then turned around to go down New Street, Woodleigh Road, back up Bridge Street and on towards the church where a service was held and a collection made of £6.

The procession was led by the Drum-Major, (Sergeant-Major Downes), followed by the Band of C Company, Yeomanry, Volunteers, Postmen, Firemen, Church Lads' Brigade, Railwaymen, Bricklayers' and Masons' Society, Working Men's Club, Gloucester Liberal Benefit Society, Foresters and finally Oddfellows. Marching with the procession were a number of collectors with their boxes marked 'In Aid of the Cottage Hospital & Dispensary' who extracted donations from the hundreds of people who had turned up to view the spectacle. Many spectators were on the upper floors of the buildings, but not even they were missed. Some collectors had a long pole on the end of which was attached a collecting bag. This was then raised aloft for contributions to be made.

After the service, the procession reformed in Worcester Road, and marched to the Market House before dispersing. The collectors then met, broke the seals on their boxes and counted the money which totalled £24.3.0d, compared to £17.16.2d the previous year, in addition to the £6 collected at the church.

The last of the Church Parade passing the Feathers Hotel on their way to Gloucester House in the Southend where they turned to come back into the town. It was not long after this that the rendering on the hotel was removed to expose the timber framing.

Bosbury Red Cross Donkey

The Bosbury Red Cross Donkey was kept by Mr. E. T. Lane at Old Court Farm, Bosbury. During the First World War, the donkey and cart would venture out fund-raising for the Red Cross in places as far apart as Ledbury, Leominster and Crickhowell. The two Misses Lane were often the nurses in the cart.

In Ledbury, the donkey and cart were put up for auction 316 times at the Ledbury and District Farmers Red Cross Jumble Sales and eventually raised over £313. Visits to Bromsgrove yielded £74, Weobley £105, Leominster £568, Hereford £250, Tenbury £533, Worcester £650 and Crickhowell £90. At the end of each outing, the place and amount raised were painted onto the cart.

The Bosbury Red Cross Donkey poses in front of the Market House. On the left of the cart is Mr. Victor Gabb dressed in lady's attire. He was the publican at No. 7, now known as The Hereford Bull. On the right is Mr. William Lewis, affectionately known as 'Old Bill'. He was well known in the district as a collector for charities. The cart was kept at Old Court Farm, Bosbury, by Mr. Lane, and is at the beginning of its fund-raising.

The Ledbury Church Fancy Fair

The Fancy Fair was held on July 15th, 1909 in the grounds of the Park in order to raise funds for the building of a Church Room. The Top Cross and the Southend were decorated with flags and bunting. In the grounds, stalls were erected near the paths, many of them with large-scale models of the half-timbered buildings in the town as a background. For example, the vegetable and produce stall was in front of a model of the old Market House, and the china and pottery stall in front of a model of Mr. George Hill's residence. The stalls were varied - fancywork, baskets, fruit and flowers, childrens, variety, advertisement, sweets, bran pies stalls - all stocked and run by local people.

In addition to the stalls were competitions for cake making, doll-dressing, making articles from materials costing less than 1/-, needlework, knitting and buttermaking. There were 'Ye Olde Shooting Range', Hoop-la, and coconut shies. Tea and refreshments were served all day.

The gross takings for the fair were £230, £180 of which went towards the Church Room building fund. The Church room was opened on November 3rd, 1910. The total cost of the building in the Cattle Market Road was £602, which included both the land and the furniture!

The vegetable and produce stall in front of Ye Olde Market Hall. Mrs. Luke Tilley, Mrs. W. P. Barry, Miss Nellie Hill, Miss Tyrrell and Miss Florrie Webb display their wares including rabbits (live and dead), home-made cakes, rhubarb and onions. The notice in the middle reads 'Your parcel delivered or taken care of by the Church Lads Brigade for 1d'.

Mrs. Jarley's Waxworks at the Ledbury Church Fancy Fair. Mr. H. G. Walker was Mrs. Jarley and Mr. J. C. Custance was Jarge. Others in the group were: Laughing Lady, Mr. J. H. Leo; two-legged girl, Miss Marjorie and Master Clifford Horton; Boy stood on the Burning Deck, Master Edward Meacham; Dwarf, Master Arthur Williams; Jack and Jill, Miss E. Townsend and Mr. T. C. Sheaf; Golden Locke, Miss G. Cotton; Babes in the Wood, Mr. R. B. Hayes and Miss Beaumont; Little Red Riding Hood, Miss Mabel Paul; Sleeping Beauty, Miss Ruby Madders; The Singing Lady, Mr. Reginald Paul; and Little Jack Horner, Master Donald Tilley. But which was which?

'The Pied Piper', November 1st-4th, 1909

Miss Bickham, who lived at Underdown, trained fifty girls to take part in six consecutive performances of 'The Pied Piper' in aid of funds for the proposed Parish Room building. Each of the performances was played to a full house. The Pied Piper was played by Mr. C. Bedford, whose 'ability was far above average' according to the local paper. The Mayor was played by Mr. J. H. Yeo, and the orchestra was led by Miss Masefield. The newspaper was equally complimentary to Miss Hilda James who played Hans. She had 'a very large part and in every particular she proved a star. Her acting was perfect.' After the last curtain call, there were shouts for Miss Bickham who appeared and was given a bouquet. The gross receipts were nearly £100 of which almost £60 went to the Parish Room building fund.

The cast of *The Pied Piper* which played to full audiences at the Royal Hall between November 1st and 4th 1909. Over fifty girls took part in a spectacle that was described by the local newspaper as 'one of the finest performances ever seen in Ledbury'. After the last performance the rats used in the play were sold as souvenirs - Daddy rats for 6d., Mummy rats for 6d. and Baby Rats for 3d.

Prams adorned with flowers in readiness for the Carnival parade about 1920. The photograph was taken at the entrance to Newbury Park in the Homend.

Disasters

Railway Accidents

Ledbury has been the scene of two railway accidents, both of which were serious in terms of damage to rolling stock, but fortunately neither involved any serious personal injury.

At about 9.30 p.m. on Saturday May 9th, 1908, a Midland Railway goods train travelling from Worcester to Swansea broke a coupling and separated in Ledbury tunnel. The engine and the first few trucks continued the journey only as far as Rea Bridge, less than a mile beyond the station, where a signal at danger brought them to a halt. Meanwhile, the rear part of the train was gathering speed through the station and down the gradient over the viaduct to plough into the back of the stationary front part. Sixteen trucks were derailed. Most of the trucks contained steel shavings and filings. Breakdown gangs from both Worcester and Hereford attended the scene and had to replace a large number of sleepers and chairs as well as rerail the train. Fortunately, nobody was injured.

The second railway accident occurred at the north end of the tunnel on a wet Sunday morning just before 4 a.m. A goods train from Wolverhampton bound for Cardiff failed to stop at a signal, ran up an emergency siding, demolished the stop block, ploughed up the soil, overturned and wrecked twelve trucks. The accident was heard all over Ledbury because many of the trucks and vans contained buckets, pots, pans and other ironmongery. The driver, Mr. Hazel from Cardiff, was pinned underneath his engine for two hours, and was freed by pulling his feet out from his boots. He was taken to the Cottage Hospital where he was treated by Dr. G. R. McKean for shock and abrasions. The fireman and guard suffered only minor bruising.

Nearly 100 men were employed clearing the wreckage and the steam crane from Swindon was used to lift the trucks and engine. Part of the embankment had to be cut away to allow enough room for the crane to work.

A truck rests in the embankment just above the main road from Ledbury to Hereford at Rea Bridge. Several black firs were felled by the derailed trucks and the signal post just beyond the workmen was broken.

The crowds have gathered to look at recovery works. The buckets and pans are dumped at the top of the bank. Hardly one escaped damage. Just behind the tender is a boiler on its way to South Wales from Cradley Heath, and the truck behind that contains bricks.

The engine proved very difficult to lift because it had become embedded in the soil and it was not possible to pass chains around it. The men with spades are making a channel underneath the engine for the chains to be passed through.

Bosbury Church Fire

At about 3.30 p.m. on July 12th 1917, one of the residents of Bosbury noticed that the vestry of the church was on fire. Alarm was immediately sent to Ledbury by telephone, and a steam fire engine under the charge of Inspector Hopkins set off for the village. The news spread almost as quickly as the fire, and a lot of the men who had been working in the fields joined the women in fetching buckets of water to dampen the flames. Nearly all the church fittings were saved by the villagers before the fire engine arrived. The Rev. H. Grindley even managed to rescue some registers dating back to 1558 which were in a charred and very hot safe.

By the time the Fire Brigade arrived, the vestry was burnt out, and the west end of the church was well alight. The firemen sprayed several jets of water onto the church from a brook close by and managed to get the fire under control. It was fortunate that the day had been still, and therefore the fire did not spread too quickly.

There was no obvious cause of the fire, and it was concluded that it was probably started by a match dropped by a visitor. The church had been open to visitors all day, and there was no attendant to show them round.

It took a long time to raise the money required to restore the church. By the end of 1922, monies had been obtained from the insurance company, from a subscription list and from special gifts and totalled £3,365. Nearly all of that money had been spent, and there were several accounts still unpaid.

Debris from the collapsed roof fills the pews. The fire damaged the walls, and some stitching and strengthening had to be undertaken. The new vestry and screen were donated by Mrs Buck and Miss Beith.

The font in the middle of the picture dates back to the twelfth century. The chains hanging from the ceiling no longer support the beautiful brass oil lamps which were used to light the church. They were rescued by the villagers before the fire brigade reached the church. The photographer has left his hat on top of the pews.

On August 27th 1912 there was extensive flooding of the River Leadon, though it is debatable whether the depth of water, clearly not above ankle-length, merits the grandiose title 'The Great Flood at Ledbury' which appears on the postcard. One of the boys is brandishing a cricket bat, hardly an appropriate sport in those weather conditions. The boy on the right has a hoop which is reflecting in the water. The house was at the bottom of Little Marcle Road, but has since been demolished.

Ledbury Fire Brigade pose with their tenders at the rear of St. Katherine's Almshouses. The Chief Officer was Mr. R. G. Gurney. During the day the alarm was the bell in St. Katherine's Chapel, and at night there was a fire alarm pillar in High Street which connected to members of the Brigade with electric bells. The Fire Brigade operated a motor trailer pump, a motor tender, steam fire engine and a hose cart. The fire station was in Church Street.

The Great War

On August 4th 1914, war was declared on Germany. The following day, the citizens of Ledbury turned out in force to say goodbye to the men of C Company, 1st Battalion Herefordshire Regiment. They hung flags and banners from the buildings and cheered and waved as the Territorial Army left the town for active service.

The eighty-three men of the Company were called up on the Tuesday. Only four of them failed to assemble at the Drill Hall on the Wednesday, and that was because they were working out of town. Captain A. V. Holman was in command as the procession left the Drill Hall in New Street to march to the railway station. They were led by a band of the 1st City of Westminster Boy Scouts, who were camping at Bosbury, and also a local brass band. They took it in turns to provide the music.

The soldiers arrived in good time to catch the 5.2 p.m. train to Hereford, where they had to change trains and continue their journey to Pembroke Dock. They filled the platform, and posed for pictures, but the townsfolk of Ledbury who had come to see them off were not so lucky. They were stopped at the booking office, although a number did climb over the railings. The crowd cheered when the train arrived, and as soon as the soldiers were on board they rushed onto the platform to wave handkerchiefs and no doubt shed a few tears.

Only one accident marred the day. A cyclist named James Parr from Stafford, who was on a cycling tour, fell off his bicycle and injured his face. He received attention at the hospital and he was later able to continue his journey.

The Church Lads Brigade also played their part in the First World War. On 20th August 1914, twenty-four lads from the Ledbury, Colwall, Wellington Heath and Eastnor Companies caught the 8 a.m. train bound for Rhyader. Their task was to patrol part of the pipeline which carried water from Rhyader to Birmingham. The Rev. Carnegy, rector of Ledbury, and his wife were amongst those to see them safely on the train. Once in Rhyader Captain Mitford divided the camp into three patrols - the nine Ledbury lads under Sergeant Davis, the nine Wellington Heath lads under Sergeant Pedlingham, and the remaining six under Sergeant Grubb of Colwall. The lads were on duty for six hours at a time.

The Territorials assemble outside the Drill Hall in New Street. There were posters all along the route to the station proclaiming 'Good luck to the Terriers', and it was no mean feat to have those posters printed and distributed in such a short time. A number of the soldiers have obviously seen the cameraman.

The band of the Westminster Boy Scouts is at the front of the march as it progresses past the Market House and through the hundreds of people who had turned out to wish the soldiers luck.

Most of the soldiers are on the train and the crowds have surged onto the platform to wave goodbye.

Members of the Church Lads Brigade pose for the camera on the station platform before departing for Rhayader. Members of the station staff have also crept into the picture. The Rev. Carnegy, rector of Ledbury, is at the back of the group.

Waste paper is left outside on the High Street ready for collection in aid of the war effort.

Around & about Ledbury

Much Marcle

Delivery time at The Walwyn Arms, Much Marcle. The beer had travelled eight miles from the Alton Court Brewery at Ross-on-Wye.

The Lodge to Homme House, Much Marcle, on the Ledbury to Ross-on-Wye road.

Much Marcle Church with the post office on the left. In the churchyard was a large yew tree in the trunk of which was carved a seat, capable of accommodating 10 people.

The postman and some of the villagers look at the photographer in Much Marcle village.

Eastnor village green and school. On the back of the postcard, posted in Jauuary, 1905 it reads: 'Reg and I are over here today skating.' Presumably it refers to the lake at the castle.

Eastnor

A very early picture of Eastnor Castle. Later additions included a new walled terrace. The castle was built by Earl Somers between 1812 and 1820 to the design of Sir Samuel Smirke and stands in 500 acres of park.

There is a fine collection of armour and paintings in the castle. This view shows the magnificence of the drawing room.

Trumpet Post Office in 1910, looking towards Hereford. Only the post office remains which is now a private house next to the garage.

Trumpet

The Old Trumpet Inn in 1916. This was a favourite meeting place for the Ledbury Hunt. The landlord was James Townsend.

The Old Lych Gate at Cradley, about eight miles from Ledbury. In the churchyard is a sundial which was erected in commemoration of Queen Victoria's Jubilee. The young ladies must have enjoyed posing for the camera because a few minutes later, the very same three went round the corner and stood outside the old boy's school, which later became the Parish Hall, whilst the photographer took another picture.

Cradley

The message on the back of this postcard reads: 'This little low building (behind where the man is standing) is the village store. Just a few shops away from the church.' The village store is still there today.

Bosbury

Bosbury village main street in the late 1920s. Sadly, most of the trees in the churchyard have now gone. The field in the distance now supports houses.

Bosbury Village Stores in 1905, where you could buy anything from butter and bacon to buckets and spades. Today the frontages of the shops have gone, and the local garage has taken their place.

It is a shame that the glass plate from which this photograph is taken is cracked, but it is very interesting in that it shows the centre of the village before the Colwall Park Hotel was built in 1905. On the left is the Post Office and W. Plowman's grocers shop. On the walls of the Post Office are posters advertising for recruits into 'His Majesty's Regular Army.'

Colwall

Colwall Park Hotel and the Old Stone in 1908. The railway station canopy can be seen in the distance. H. Percy Smith, an architect from Worcester, is superintending some building work going on at the back of the hotel.

On the Ledbury road just approaching Colwall Green. The horse and cart belong to V. W. Meacham, chemists in High Street, Ledbury. Besides dispensing medicines, Mr. Meacham was also an agent for Schweppe & Co.'s Mineral Waters, and the delivery cart is no doubt on its return journey from the Schweppe's depot on the other side of the village.

Evendine, Colwall, on the road leading from Colwall Green to Jubilee Drive near British Camp. The house on the right remains almost the same, but the other two cottages have lost their thatch and have been altered in appearance.

Family Grocer.

The Cheapest and Best in Ledbury.

Provision Merchant.

Frederick W. Taylor,

19, High Street,

LEDBURY.

F. W. TAYLOR is specially noted for his DELICIOUS WILTSHIRE MILD BACON & HAMS, and all GROCERIES.

Tea Dealer.

Corn Dealer.

TILLEY & SON,

Photographic Post Card Specialists.

WE PHOTOGRAPH

Any Local View, Private Residence, Shop Front, School Groups, Trade Designs, Animals, Portrait, &c., &c.,

And supply POST CARDS from same at the following

LOW PRICES.

12 REAL PHOTO POST CARDS FOR 2/6.
Best Quality, 3/6.
100 REAL PHOTO POST CARDS FOR 12/6.
200 COLLOTYPE POST CARDS FOR 15/-.
250 FOR 17/6. 500 FOR 20/-. 1,000 FOR 25/-.

The above Prices include taking the Photograph.
Send for Specimens.

We publish over **400** different Local View Post Cards of Ledbury and District.

TILLEY & SON, Photographers, Ledbury.

Feathers Hotel,

Family and Commercial:
LEDBURY.

Proprietor: - - T. HOWELL.

BILLIARDS.

Head-Quarters Cyclist's Touring . . . . and Automobile Clubs.

Posting in all its Branches.
Accommodation for Hunters, &c.
Hearse and Mourning Carriages.
Garage, and Motor Cars on Hire.

Large and Spacious Ball and Assembly Room and Ante-Rooms.

Omnibus meets all Trains. **Tariff on Application.**

THE LEDBURY MARKETS AND FAIRS Co., Ltd.

ALL PAYMENTS TO BE MADE UPON ENTERING THE MARKET.

LEDBURY MARKET TOLLS.

STOCK SALES HELD ON ALTERNATE TUESDAYS, Commencing Jan. 7, 1908.

Horses	each 6d.	Calves under 12 months	each 2d.
Colts under 3 years ...	„ 3d.	Sheep and Lambs ...	„ 1d.
Cattle	„ 3d.	Pigs	„ 1d.
Bulls (to be tied up) ...	„ 6d.	„ Sucking ...	„ ½d.

Fruit per Pot, 1d.

N.B.—The above Tolls for Stock include the use of any of the Pens on the Market.

Manager and Secretary:
HENRY GARROOD, Solicitor, Ledbury.

Tea & Coffee always Ready.

M. Clarke & A. Amyes,

33, HOMEND STREET, LEDBURY,
Near the Corner of Bank Crescent,

Have a Good Supply of . .

TRIPE & COWHEELS at Moderate Prices on MONDAYS & FRIDAYS.

Also

WHITE & BLACK PUDDINGS,
FRESH FAGGOTS, &c.,
Constantly on Sale.

W. H. HATTON & SON,

OIL, COLOURS, VARNISHES, &c., of the best quality.

GLASS, TILES, & SLATES always in stock.

Builders, Sanitary Plumbers, & House Decorators,
NEW STREET, LEDBURY.

Paper-Hangings in great variety. Prompt attention to orders in every branch.

Established over Half a Century.

Carriages, Carts, and Motor Body Work of all descriptions to order.

Carriages Let on Hire, also Bought and Sold on Commission.

George Hopkins & Sons,

CARRIAGE & MOTOR WORKS,

New Street, LEDBURY.

Repairs, Painting, Trimming, and Leather Work Neatly Executed at the . . . . . . Most Reasonable Charges.

Personal Superintendence. *Workmanship Guaranteed.*

"Wired-on," "Royal Sirdar Buffer," and "Clincher" Solid Rubber Tyres, fitted on the Premises, to old or new Wheels of Carriages and Motor Cars.

Wheels Re-Rubbered in a few Hours.
Michelin Motor Tyres in Stock. Petrol and Motor Lubricants.

Carriage Lamps, Candles, India Rubber Mats, Brake Blocks, and everything connected with the trade.

ESTIMATES FREE.

GEORGE HILL,

Building Contractor,

Homend Street, Ledbury.

Retailer of Building Materials of all kinds.
White Sawdust always in Stock.

STEAM JOINERY WORKS.
Skilled Workmen in every Branch of the Building Trade.

SANITARY WORK Carried out on most Modern Principles.
Drains Tested and Reported Upon.

Brass, Lead, & Iron Pumps. Hot & Cold Water Fitting. Ranges, Baths, Lavatories, Water Closets, Radiators, and Plumber's Work in General by Registered Certificated Plumber.

Glazing, Painting, - - - - - - and Paperhanging.

WALL PAPERS Extensively Stocked.

Plain & Ornamental Wrought Ironwork Gates, Railings, & General Smith's Work.

PLANS PREPARED.
Buildings Surveyed and Reported Upon.
Estimates Given.
Charges Strictly Moderate.

BUILDER OF:
The Ledbury Cottage Hospital.
The Barrett Browning Memorial.
The Royal Hall (at the Royal Oak Hotel.
Colwall & Ashperton Railway Stations.
Evendine Court, Colwall.
New Board Room and Offices, Workhouse, Ross.

Agent for the "Drawwell" Grate, placed first at the New Government Offices in the final test.

Established Half a Century.

A Large and Varied Stock of Ladies', Gentlemen's and Children's Boots and Shoes Carefully Selected from the Best London, Stafford, Northampton, and Paris Houses.

REPAIRS Neatly and Promptly Executed.

W. HAMPTON & SON,

Family Boot and Shoe Makers,
Upper Cross, LEDBURY.

Hunting & Livery Boots Made to Order.

All kinds of LADIES' & GENT'S BOOTS & SHOES Made to Order on Anatomical and Hygienic Principles.

Sole Agents for the - - - WATERPROOF "K" BOOTS

Scafe's Patent Leather and Rubber Combination Boots, and the Flexible Boots